CUTE & EASY

Boys!

CAKE TOPPERS

CW00501493

Contributors

Following a career in finance, Amanda Mumbray launched her cake business in 2010 and has gone from strength to strength, delighting customers with her unique bespoke creations and winning several Gold medals at various International Cake Shows. Amanda's **Clever Little Cupcake** company is based near Manchester, UK: www.cleverlittlecupcake.co.uk

Amanda Mumbray

Angela Morrison grew up in Venezuela around a wide variety of food and desserts, but it was when she moved to Virginia Beach, Va that her business **'Cakes by Angela Morrison'** was born. She has a wide online following for her super cute cake topper creations and her work has been published in many cake magazines and blogs.

Angela Morrison

Helen Penman has been designing cakes for over 15 years and her work has been featured in a wide range of cake books and magazines. She has also written several cake decorating and modelling books of her own, and runs a successful cake company from her home in Kent, UK.
www.toonicetoslice.co.uk

Helen Penman

Naomi from Calgary, Alberta-based **'Tea Party Cakes'** found her passion for cake decorating in 2010 when she took a course at a local craft store, and her work has since been featured in a host of cake magazines and websites. Naomi is also a regular contributor to *SugarEd Productions Online School*.

Naomi Hubert

First published in 2015 by Kyle Craig Publishing

Text and illustration copyright © 2015 Kyle Craig Publishing

Editor: Alison McNicol

Design and illustration: Julie Anson

ISBN: 978-1-908707-62-8

A CIP record for this book is available from the British Library.

A Kyle Craig Publication

www.kyle-craig.com

Contents

Welcome!

Welcome to '**Cute & Easy Cake Toppers for BOYS!**', the latest title in the **Cute & Easy Cake Toppers** Collection.

Each book in the series focuses on a specific theme, and this book contains a gorgeous selection of beautiful cake toppers perfect for any little boy's birthday party or celebration!

Whether you're an absolute beginner or an accomplished cake decorator, these projects are suitable for all skill levels, and we're sure that you will have as much fun making them as we did!

Enjoy!

Fondant/Sugarpaste/Gumpaste

Fondant/Sugarpaste – Ready-made fondant, also called ready to roll icing, is widely available in a selection of fantastic colours. Most regular cake decorators find it cheaper to buy a larger quantity in white and mix their own colours using colouring pastes or gels. Fondant is used to cover entire cakes, and as a base to make modelling paste for modelling and figures (see below).

Modelling Paste – Used throughout this book. Firm but pliable and dries faster and harder than fondant/sugarpaste. When making models, fondant can be too soft so we add CMC/Tylose powder to thicken it.

Florist Paste/Gumpaste – The large and small shoes in this book are made using florist paste as it is more pliable than fondant, but dries very quickly and becomes quite hard, so it is widely used for items like flowers that are delicate but need to hold their shape when dry.

Florist Paste can be bought ready made, or you can make at home by adding Gum-Tex/Gum Tragacanth to regular fondant.

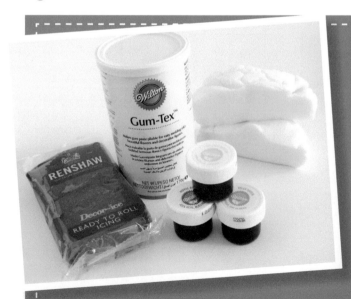

How to Make Modelling Paste

Throughout this book we refer to 'paste', meaning modelling paste. You can convert regular shop-bought fondant into modelling paste by adding CMC/Tylose powder, which is a thickening agent.

Add approx 1 tsp of CMC/Tylose powder to 225g (8oz) of fondant/sugarpaste. Knead well and leave in an airtight freezer bag for a couple of hours.

Add too much and it will crack. If this happens, add in a little shortening (white vegetable fat) to make it pliable again.

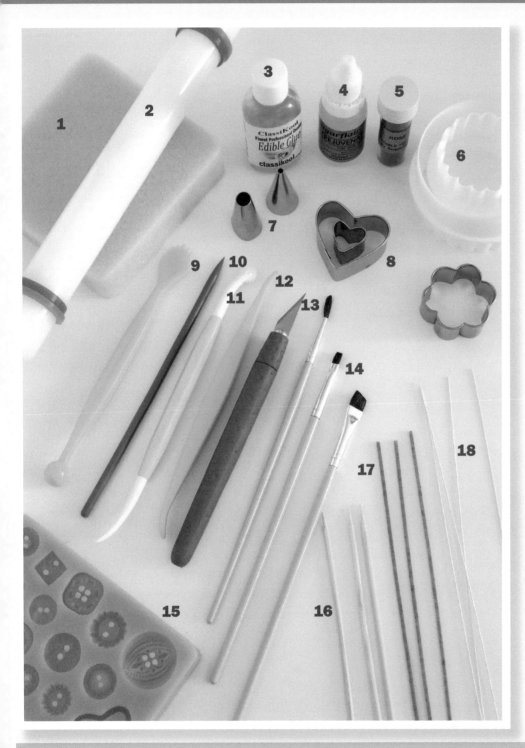

1 Foam Pad – holds pieces in place while drying.

2 Rolling pin – acrylic works better than wooden when working with fondant/paste.

3 Edible glue – essential when creating models. See below.

4 Rejuvenator spirit – mix with food colourings to create an edible paint.

5 Petal Dust, pink – for adding a 'blush' effect to cheeks.

6 Round and scalloped cutters – a modelling essential.

7 Piping nozzles – used to shape mouths and indents.

8 Shaped cutters – various uses.

9 Ball tool/serrated tool – another modelling essential.

10 Small pointed tool – used to create details like nostrils and holes.

11 Quilting tool – creates a stitched effect.

12 Veining tool – for adding details to flowers and models.

13 Craft knife/scalpel – everyday essential.

14 Brushes – to add finer details to faces.

15 Moulds – create detailed paste buttons, fairy wings and lots more.

16 Wooden skewers – to support larger models.

17 Spaghetti strands – also used for support.

18 Coated craft wire – often used in flower making.

Edible Glue

Whenever we refer to 'glue' in this book, we of course mean 'edible glue'. You can buy bottles of edible glue, which is strong and great for holding larger models together. You can also use a light brushing of water, some royal icing, or make your own edible glue by dissolving ¼ teaspoon tylose powder in 2 tablespoons warm water. Leave until dissolved and stir until smooth. This will keep for up to a week in the refrigerator.

Making Faces

The faces featured in this book vary in terms of detail and difficulty. If you're a complete beginner, you may opt to use simple shapes and edible pens to draw on simple features. As your confidence grows, you can use fondant for eyes and pupils, edible paint for features, or combine these methods for some great detailing.

A veining tool will create indents for features.

Pink petal dust adds blush to cheeks.

Various colours of paste can be layered to create detailed eyes.

Edible pens can be used to draw on simple features.

A tiny ball of paste can create a nose.

Black fondant with white fondant or non-pareils make detailed eyes.

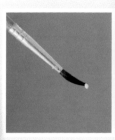
When adding tiny pieces of fondant for eyes, use a moist fine brush.

When making small figures for cupcakes, it's great to place each on a topper disc, and place this on top of a lovely swirl of buttercream. This way the figure can be removed and kept, and the child can tuck into the main cupcake.

Regular round cutters are essentials, and there are also a great selection of embossing tools and sheets out there that, when pressed into your rolled paste, will create cool quilting effects on your disc. Make your discs first and allow them to harden before you fix your figures to them.

Some figures may use a toothpick or skewer for support, so be sure to take care with these around small children.

Plunger cutters are a great way to add cute details to your models. They cut and then 'push' each small piece out, making it easy to cut small flowers, leaves and shapes.

Painting Details

Many of the projects in this book have beautiful details painted onto the mini items. Mixing regular gel or paste food colouring, or lustre dusts, with rejuvenator spirit will create edible paint in any colour you need. Keep a small collection of fine paintbrushes handy too!

Coloured details – mix your regular food colouring with rejuvenator spirit to create edible paint.

White paint – Americolor Bright White gel paste colour is strong enough to paint on clear white details.

Fireman Cake

1 First let's make our friendly fireman!

2 Roll a thick sausage and make a cut down the middle to make the legs.

3 Shape the legs with your hands, and mark on creases with the veining tool. Insert a bamboo skewer down one leg, and snip off the end.

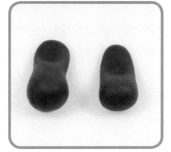

4 Roll two small sausages and flatten at one end.

5 Attach the shoes to the bottom of each trouser leg.

6 Roll a teardrop shape for the body, and insert over the exposed bamboo skewer.

7 Mark a line up the front of his tunic, and add a little ball of paste for the collar. Insert a toothpick for the head.

8 Roll two tapered sausages for the arms, creasing with the veining tool at the elbow. Open up the end with the cone tool.

9 Bend a piece of florist wire, carefully thread one of the arms over the wire, and snip off the excess with wire cutters.

10 Attach both of the arms to the body, leaving a little bit of wire at the end of the wired arm poking out.

11 Roll a ball of paste for the head, slightly indenting at the centre.

12 For the hands, roll out a teardrop shape, flatten slightly, and make cuts as shown to make the fingers.

13 Attach the hands to the figure.

14 Using the ball tool, make two eye sockets, and mark a mouth shape with the end of a piping tip.

15 Open up the mouth with the veining tool.

16 Fill the mouth with a little amount of pink paste.

17 Add a tiny sausage of paste for the teeth and fill the eye sockets with little balls of paste. Add two tiny indented balls for the ears.

18 Paint the eyes in, and dust the cheeks with a little petal dust.

19 For the hat, roll a pear shape, pinch out the bottom to make a brim, and use the ball tool to hollow out the inside slightly.

20 Cut a small strip and attach to the top of the hat.

21 Attach two small circles of paste to make the badge.

22 Attach the hat to the head.

23 Roll three teardrop shapes for the hair and arrange around the head.

24 Now let's make this little fireman a truck to drive!

25 Stack the rice krispies into a rectangle like this, and secure with a little sugar glue. Leave the glue to set for about 15-20 minutes.

26 When set, cut away the shape, as shown, with a serrated knife.

27 Cover the whole structure in red paste, and mark on the basic details, as shown, with a veining tool.

28 Cut a long strip of black paste, and attach to the bottom of the engine.

29 Cut four circles for the wheels and attach.

30 Add a little grey circle for the wheel centres.

31 Cut out red circles, and cut them into quarters. Attach two of the quarters to each wheel.

32 Hand cut the windscreen and side windows using a craft knife. Attach tiny strips for the door handles.

33 Add two blue circles to the door and rear side.

34 Attach two little stars inside the blue circles.

35 Cut then mark some ribbed lines for the grey shutter panels, as shown, and cut pieces to fit the side of the engine.

36 Roll little sausages for the handles.

37 Attach two flattened teardrop shapes on top for the flashing lights.

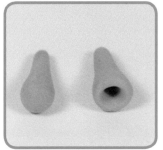

38 Roll two teardrop shapes for the horns, opening them up at the ends with the cone tool.

39 Attach a flattened ball of paste in between the lights and arrange the horns either side.

40 Cut a thin strip of yellow and attach just beneath the front window.

41 Cut out a rectangular shape to make the front grill, and add some ribbed lines.

42 Attach a thick piece of white for the bumper.

43 Mark the headlights and extra details on the bumper with your veining tool.

44 Cut some strips and attach to the centre of the bumper.

45 Roll out some yellow modelling paste and cut three squares from it.

46 Using your craft knife, cut along the sides to make the ladder. Attach it to the top of the engine.

Dinosaur Cake

Materials

Modelling paste:
Blue
Yellow
Green
White
Edible pen: black
Petal dust: pink
Edible glue

Tools

Craft knife/scalpel
Veining tool
Toothpicks
Round piping tip (# 4)
Rose leaf plunger cutters
Fine paintbrush

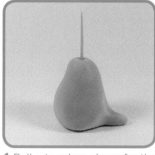

1 Roll a teardrop shape for the body, and pull out a little tail at the back. Insert a toothpick ready to take the head.

2 Roll out two sausage shapes. Roll in the middle, flatten the top end, and pinch out a foot with your fingers.

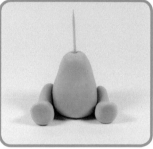

3 Attach the legs to the body with edible glue.

4 Cut a section for the chest, marking with a veining tool. Cut two circles for the paws, and three tiny circles with the end of a piping tip for the toe pads.

5 Roll out two small tapered sausages for the arms and secure to the body.

6 Add a large pear shaped ball of paste for the head, and make two holes for the nostrils with the end of a paintbrush.

7 Cut a frill and attach to the back.

8 Cut out a few different sized circles to make the spots on the back.

9 Paint on the facial details with an edible pen, and dust the cheeks with a little petal dust. Add a couple of tiny indented ball shapes for the ears.

10 Roll two tiny white cones for the horns and attach in between ears.

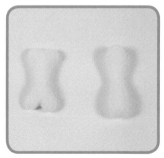

11 Roll out a sausage shape, indenting slightly in the middle. With the veining tool, push it in to the end of the bone to make the bone shape.

12 Roll out egg shapes.

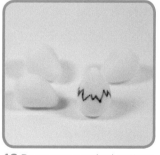

13 Draw on a cracked pattern to one of the eggs using the edible marker.

14 Cut out a few different sized leaves using the plunger cutters.

13

Boat Cake

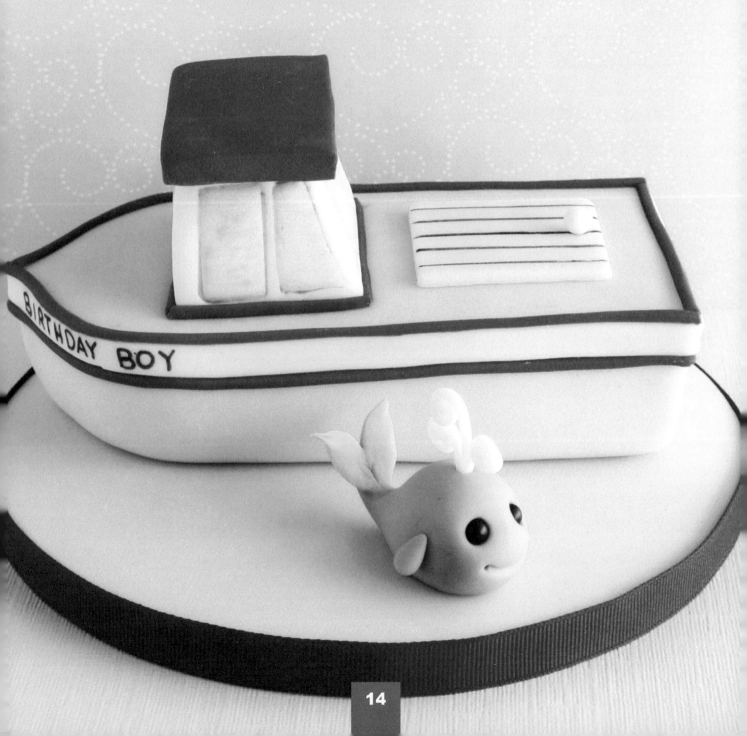

Materials

Modelling paste:
Light blue
Red
White
Grey
4mm black sugar pearls
Rice Krispie Bars
Petal dust: pink
Food colour: blue
Edible pen: black
Rejuvenator spirit
Edible glue

Tools

Craft knife/scalpel
6" cake board, covered (optional)
Piping tip
Strip cutters, 3mm & 7mm
Paint brush, small
Toothpicks

1 Draw a boat and cabin template, in the size you require, onto parchment paper. Cut and place on the Rice Krispie Bars and cut out using a sharp knife.

2 Trim the bottom of the boat to round it out. Trim the top of the cabin so that it is narrower than the bottom on one side.

3 Flip the boat so that it is bottom up. Cover with blue paste and trim away any excess.

4 Roll more blue paste and place the boat top down on it. Cut around, then fix to top of boat using edible glue.

5 Cut white strips of paste and thinner strips of red paste and attach to sides of boat with edible glue.

6 Cover the cabin of the boat with white paste and trim off any excess.

7 Mark the side windows with a rectangle cutter and/or a knife. Paint each window lightly with blue gel colour mixed with rejuvenator spirit (or vodka).

8 Cut out a medium square of white paste, adding details with the black edible pen, plus a small ball for handle.

9 Cut a thick rectangle of red paste for the cabin roof and secure with edible glue.

10 Roll some grey paste into a teardrop shape, bending the narrow end up into a tail.

11 Flatten the narrow end of the tear drop and cut a small triangle in the middle. Lightly pinch each fin with your fingers.

12 Add black sugar pearls, or small balls of paste, for eyes, and mark the mouth with the wide end of a piping tip and a toothpick.

13 Indent a blowhole with the end of paintbrush and roll and curl three thin sausages to create the water spurt. Roll two tiny grey tear drops for the front fins.

14 Brush cheeks with pink petal dust and position everything either on a covered cake board as shown, or directly onto your cake.

Boat Cupcakes

1 Cut out the desired number of plain topper discs and set aside to dry.

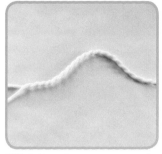

2 Twist two long sausages of white paste into a rope and arrange on a topper disc.

3 To make the anchor, cut out a small circle of grey fondant and use a piping tip to cut a circle from the middle.

4 Cut out a slivered moon shape as shown, then cut the three strips for the body of the anchor.

5 Allow pieces to dry then glue in place on top of the rope, with another small piece of rope coiled around, as shown in step 1.

6 For the numbered toppers, make more rope in the same way, and glue around the edge of the disc.

7 Roll out red paste thinly and cut out the number. Place in the centre of the disc.

8 Roll white paste thickly, cut a circle then a smaller circle from the centre. Use your finger to round out the edges.

9 Roll and cut red paste strips, and glue in place as shown.

10 Brush the back with water or edible glue and attach to topper disc.

11 To make the sail boat, roll and cut out a circle of red paste, then cut in half.

12 Roll and cut out a white diamond shape. Cut into sections for the sails, as shown.

13 Arrange and attach the pieces on the disc as shown. Add a thin white strip and a tiny blue star.

14 Follow the Steps 10 to 14 of the Boat Cake Topper to create the little whale.

17

Airplane Cake

Materials

Modelling paste:
Red
Yellow
Black
Brown
Flesh
White
Petal dust: pink
Edible glue

Tools

Craft knife/scalpel
Veining tool
Flower cutter
Circle cutters
Fine paintbrush
Toothpicks

1 Roll a long tapered sausage and hollow out a cockpit, either with your fingers or a large ball tool.

2 Cut out the wing shapes, and also two circles. Cut one of the circles in half, and the other just more than half, as shown.

3 Attach the wings to the plane, supporting them with foam until dry. Use the larger semi circle for the top tail, and the two equal half circles for the sides of the tail.

4 Use a flower cutter for the propeller. Flatten then indent a little ball of paste for the centre.

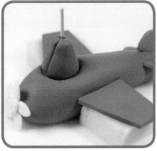

5 Roll out a small teardrop shape of paste and insert a toothpick all the way through the body and into the plane.

6 Roll out two tapered sausages for the arms, and insert two flatten balls for the hands.

7 Add a small flattened ball for the neck, and a large ball for the head. Attach a very small ball of paste for the nose.

8 Cut out a thin strip for the scarf, making small fine cuts at either end. Arrange around his neck.

9 Attach a brown paste circle to his head to make the hat.

10 Cut out a rounded oblong for the goggles, and indent at the bridge of the nose with a veining tool. Make indentations all around the edge.

11 Attach a thin strip all the way around the head for the goggle strap.

12 Paint on some detail and dust the cheeks with petal dust.

13 Roll out lots of differently sized balls and arrange randomly.

14 Wet the surface of the balls, and cover with a thin layer of paste, pushing it in to the gaps to give the cloud some definition.

Scooting Fun!

Materials

Modelling paste:
Blue
Red
Yellow
Flesh brown
Black
Grey
White
Tiny silver balls (edible)
Petal dust: pink
Edible paint: white
Edible glue

Tools

Craft knife/scalpel
Round cake board (optional)
Veining tool
Cone tool
Ball tool
Quilting wheel
Fine paintbrush
Number cutters
Bamboo skewers
18 gauge florist wire
Wire cutters/strong scissors

1 Let's start by making some cool skate themed cake or cupcake toppers. Prepare any cupcake topper discs and set aside to dry.

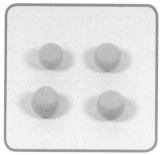

2 Roll four small balls and flatten slightly.

3 Snip a toothpick into small pieces, and carefully attach the balls to the ends.

4 Glue a tiny silver ball in the centre on each ball.

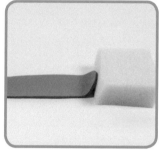

5 Cut a strip for the board, and let one end dry so it is sticking up. Leave it to dry completely.

6 Glue the board to the wheels. What a cute little skateboard!

7 Now for a cute baseball cap.

8 Roll a ball of paste and flatten on one side. Use the quilting wheel to mark the detail.

9 Cut a brim using a craft knife and stitch the edge of the shape.

10 Attach the brim to the cap, slightly pinching the brim in the centre. Attach a little ball of paste to the top.

11 Roll a very fine sausage of paste and manipulate it into your chosen letter.

12 Let's have some tunes!

13 Carefully shape a piece of grey paste into a rectangular shape.

14 Make two circles for the speakers and score on some details as shown.

15 Cut a little square for the tape deck, and score to add some detail.

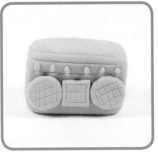

16 Roll tiny little balls of paste for the knobs.

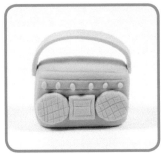

17 Cut a thin strip and attach at either end to make the handle.

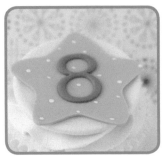

18 How old is your birthday boy?

19 Roll out some paste and cut out a star shape, one for each number cupcake.

20 Use your number cutters to cut out your desired number.

21 Attach the pieces together, and secure onto the disc, painting on a few polka dots.

22 Now let's make our boy on a scooter. It may be easier to place him on a covered cake board than directly onto the cake.

23 Cover a cake drum, and mark where you want the front of the scooter to be. Add a little rectangle of paste for the scooter to sit on.

24 Roll some paste around the bamboo skewer, leaving the pointed end exposed.

25 Position the skewer at the front of the scooter area and hammer it in to the cake drum. Trim so only a small end is now exposed.

26 Cut a small length of floristry wire, and attach to the top of the skewer, as the handlebar, securing with floristry tape.

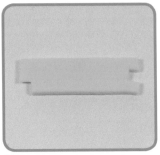

27 Cut a rectangular piece of paste, and remove little sections as shown, so the wheels will sit flush with the scooter.

28 Paint the exposed floristry tape to match the handle bars, and add little sausages of black for the handles. Attach the base of the scooter.

29 Cut two wheels, and indent the centre of each wheel with a smaller circle cutter. Attach them to the scooter.

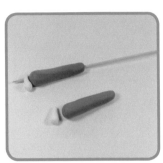

30 Roll out two tapered sausages for the legs, and two teardrop shapes for the feet. Thread one through a skewer.

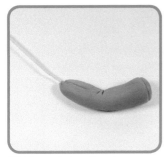

31 Thread the other leg through a bent piece of floristry wire.

32 Attach the skewered leg to the centre of the scooter, and bang it in the cake board with the end of your rolling pin.

33 Attach the other leg by taping it to the upright skewer, and attach a little foot. Mark any details on to the trousers.

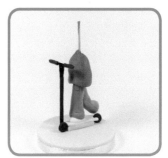

34 Roll out a teardrop shape for the body and insert it over the exposed skewer/wire.

35 Attach a ball of paste for the head, indenting slightly in the middle.

36 Using the ball tool, mark out the eye sockets, and indent the mouth. Add little balls for the ears and nose.

37 Add little balls for the eyes, and open up the mouth with a veining tool.

38 Fill in the mouth with a little pink, and a tiny sausage of white for the teeth.

39 Paint in the facial details and dust the cheeks with a little petal dust.

40 Roll two tapered sausages for the arms, marking on elbow creases with a veining tool.

41 Make two teardrop shapes, and cut away a small section to make the thumb. Mark on the fingers with a veining tool.

42 Attach the hands and arms, arranging them on the scooter.

43 Roll out a ball of paste and indent in the middle to make a hood shape.

44 Manipulate then glue the cup shape on the body to make it look like a hood.

45 Attach two little sausages of paste for the hoodie tassels.

46 Cut a piece of paste for the hair and mark with a veining tool.

Racing Car Cake

Materials

Modelling paste:
Green, light & dark
Grey
Red
White
Black
Edible pen: black

Tools

Craft knife/scalpel
Large round cake board
Ball tool
Veining tool
Rolling pin

1 Cover your cake with grass green fondant and, if desired, also cover a large round cake board to sit it on.

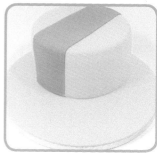

2 Roll and cut a long grey rectangle, and glue over the cake at an angle, trimming the ends neatly.

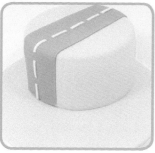

3 Roll and cut thin white stripes and glue down the centre of the 'road'. Secure in place using edible glue.

4 Roll large and small blobs of dark and light green paste and texture the paste to look like bushes and shrubs.

5 Position these on the top of the cake around the road, securing in place with edible glue.

6 Shape red paste into a flattened cylinder, then into a diamond shape. Indent the cab section with the ball tool.

7 Shape black paste into a small helmet then use a pinch of white paste for the visor.

8 Roll thin white strips and position over the car front as shown. Glue in place and trim.

9 Shape four wheels from black paste.

10 Roll two small red balls, then glue in place for the tail fin support.

11 Roll and cut a red rectangle, cutting sides at a slight angle as shown.

12 Roll and add some thin white strips to the fin, as shown.

13 Position the car onto the road on the cake, securing in place with edible glue.

14 Make the 'START' line on the road from white paste, either drawing or adding black paste squares to create the chequered effect.

Racing Car Cupcakes

Materials

Modelling paste:
Green, light & dark
Red
Blue
White
Black
Edible pen: black

Tools

Craft knife/scalpel
Ball tool
Veining tool
Quilting wheel
Pizza wheel
Toothpicks
Rolling pin

1 Roll out green paste and cut a round topper disc for each cupcake you are making.

2 It's always tastier to pipe a swirl of buttercream on each cupcake – then the child can remove and keep the car topper disc!

3 Shape red paste into a tear-drop shape, flatten the front and indent the cockpit with the ball tool.

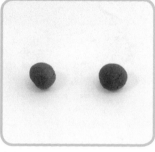

4 Roll two small red balls, supports for the wing, and glue onto the back of the car.

5 Roll and cut red paste to create the fin. Cut a rectangle and gently push into the wing shape.

6 Roll and cut some very thin white stripes and secure onto the tail wing using edible glue.

7 Secure the tail wing onto the tail struts, tilting down-wards towards the cockpit.

8 Take a pinch of black paste and shape into the helmet. Place in the cockpit hole previously made and secure with edible glue.

9 Add a small, flat white visor to the helmet.

10 Attach more thin white strips to the front nose of the racing car, using edible glue.

11 Shape four wheels from black paste – rolling and flattening four balls. Attach to the car using edible glue.

12 Roll and cut a flag and add detail with quilting wheel, then insert toothpick. If desired a name could be imprinted onto the flag.

13 Alternatively print or cut some flag shapes in colours to match the cars, with the name of the party guests.

14 Place the racing car onto the cupcake, and add any flags using toothpicks as support!

Superhero Cupcakes

28

Materials

Modelling paste:
Yellow
Black
Blue
Red
White
Edible pen: black
Edible glue

Tools

Craft knife/scalpel
Round cutters, set
Star cutter
Teardrop cutters
Rolling pin

1 Take 4 round cutters from your set and cut red discs using the largest then the second smallest circle.

2 Roll and cut a blue circle from the smallest circle cutter, then cut and add a star shape to this.

3 Finally cut a white circle from the second largest cutter and stick on top of largest red circle as shown.

4 Layer and glue all the parts as shown.

5 Roll and cut a red topper disc using medium round cutter.

6 Use the edible pen to draw in the web design as shown. Start with crossed lines, then fill in the wavy lines between them.

7 Roll out and cut two black teardrops and two slightly smaller ones.

8 Layer as shown and glue in place.

9 Roll and cut a yellow topper disc using medium round cutter.

10 Roll a long black thin sausage. Glue it to the edge of the yellow circle and trim excess.

11 Draw or find online a bat logo template and use a craft knife to cut it from black paste. Glue it to the yellow circle.

12 Draw or find online an "S" template and use a craft knife to carefully cut - around the outside only - from yellow paste.

13 Now use the same "S" template to cut out the detailed red 'S' shape.

14 Layer this onto the yellow piece then glue onto a blue topper disc.

Materials

Modelling paste:
Yellow
Black
Blue, dark & light
Red
White
Edible pen: black
Edible paint: black
Edible glue

Tools

Craft knife/scalpel
Round cutters, set
Letter & number cutters
Medium flower cutter
Fine paintbrush

1 Roll cupcake topper discs in a selection of colours – one per cupcake.

2 Roll and cut a cloud shape, using a craft knife. Make two.

3 Sketch various random 'flash' shapes on paper, then cut out a couple as templates. Use a craft knife to cut out a selection of these.

4 Cut some smaller than others so that both colours are seen when you layer them.

5 Play around with layering various options, then when happy glue the layers together.

6 Then place them onto cupcake topper discs, as shown.

7 Use the letter cutters to punch out the sayings. Glue the letters to the discs.

8 Also make some using the initial, or name, and age of the birthday boy!

9 Roll out white paste and cut out flowers to form clouds. Trim to make smaller clouds too.

10 Glue the clouds to the circles.

11 Use a fine paintbrush and black gel, or an edible pen, to paint dots on the bubble.

12 Write Happy Birthday on a large cloud topper.

13 Paint extra details on clouds using a paintbrush and black gel.

14 Finish painting the details onto the rest of the clouds.

Train Cake

Materials

Modelling paste:
Blue
Sky blue
Black
Grey
Red
Brown
White

Tools

Craft knife/scalpel
Veining tool
Small round cutter

1 Cover your cake, and if you are making matching cup-cakes to display with the cake also cover a large cake board for it to sit on.

2 Roll and cut some thick brown paste 'sleepers' and add wood effect markings with veining tool. Glue to cake.

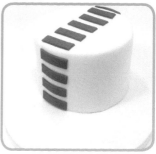

3 Roll and cut two very thin, long ribbons of black paste and attach to the sleepers with edible glue.

4 For the base of the train, form a thick grey rectangle of paste.

5 Roll, cut and add a flat rectangle of red paste on top, scoring a line across it near one edge.

6 Cut out 6 round wheels and attach to the sides of the base. Add and flatten a small round ball to each wheel.

7 Roll and crop a cylinder of paste for the boiler area and glue onto the base just along from one end.

8 Shape the cab and coalbox, dome the top and secure behind the boiler as shown.

9 Shape a black paste cylinder for the front and add a pinch of black for the chimney top.

10 Roll and cut a black rectangle and drape over the cab. Add some little black balls of 'coal' in the coalbox.

11 Shape the face from a round grey disc, ball for nose, and indent the mouth with the end of a circle cutter.

12 Use flattened white then black balls to make the eye-balls. Glue in place.

13 Roll and cut some thin red strips of paste for the stripe decoration around the cab and over the boiler.

14 Do the same to decorate another blue rectangle, then attach to the side of the boiler.

Train Cupcakes

Materials

Modelling paste:
Blue
Sky blue
Green
Black
Grey
Red
Brown
White
Edible glue

Tools

Craft knife/scalpel
Veining tool
Round cutters

1 Shape some little clouds from white paste and mark with veining tool.

2 Roll and cut one blue topper disc for each cupcake, and attach a cloud to the 'train' toppers using edible glue.

3 Cut a train outline shape like the one shown, and place on a topper disc.

4 Roll and cut a black strip, curving it slightly and place on the top of the red outline.

5 Roll and flatten two black balls for the buffers and attach to the base of the red train.

6 Roll and cut a thinner grey strip and lay above the buffers.

7 Add a black rectangle onto the train outline, gluing in place.

8 Roll and flatten two yellow balls and attach to represent the front headlights.

9 Shape grey paste for the train face, and attach to the black rectangle.

10 Indent the grey face with the back of a piping nozzle cutter, to create a smiling mouth.

11 Shape a pinch of grey paste for the nose.

12 Roll and flatten small balls of white then black paste to make the eyes. Glue in place.

13 Roll a brown rectangle, removing a semi-circle at each end with the back of a piping nozzle.

14 Mark a line down each long side of the track. Add some dark brown, textured wooden boards, as shown in main photo.

Name Train Cupcakes

Materials

Modelling paste:
Yellow
Green
Blue
Bright pink
Black
White
Edible glue

Tools

Craft knife/scalpel
Veining tool
Pizza wheel
Spaghetti strand
Square cutter

1 Shape a rectangle for the base of each train, pinching the edges to sharpen them.

2 Roll a cylinder to make the boiler, chopping to blunt the ends.

3 Roll another cylinder for the cab, and place both on train base, as shown.

4 Roll a piece for the roof and drape over the top of the cab, gluing in place.

5 Roll some paste thinly for the window, score across it with the scalpel then attach to the cab with edible glue.

6 Shape a cone from the blue for the funnel, add white paste for the 'steam' and secure with edible glue and a piece of spaghetti for support.

7 Shape and score some paste for the front 'snow clearer' and attach to the front of the train.

8 Shape four small and two large wheels from black paste. Roll into a ball and flatten. Cut green circles to fit inside and indent as shown.

9 Take a pinch of bright pink and shape into a dome, attach to the front of the train.

10 The carriages are all made the same way but with different colours. Start with the train base, as before.

11 Make a platform to fit on the base.

12 Shape 4 wheels in the same way as train wheels.

13 Attach the wheels to the sides of the carriage using edible glue.

14 Cut out each letter of the child's name from thick paste and allow to dry before securing one letter to each carriage.

Football Cupcakes

Materials

Modelling paste:
Choose paste in your team colours
Edible paint: white
Edible pen: black
Edible glue

Tools

Craft knife/scalpel
Veining tool
Fine paintbrush
FPC football mould

1 Choose paste in the birthday boy's team colours!

2 Draw a template of a jersey shape like this, and use a craft knife to cut shapes from rolled modelling paste.

3 Cut out a thin strip and attach to the collar and edges of the sleeves, marking the ribbed pattern with a veining tool.

4 Paint on some detail with food colouring or edible pens.

5 Now for some matching shorts.

6 Hand cut a pair of shorts like this using a craft knife.

7 Mark on some details with a veining tool.

8 Now for some cute soccer socks!

9 Cut out a pair of socks like this with a craft knife.

10 Cut a strip of paste to make the turnovers in the socks, and mark the ribbing with a veining tool.

11 Paint on a little logo.

12 Now for the ball. We used a special mould from FPC, but you can form from paste and add details with a veining tool.

13 Start with a plain white football shape - add details if you are not using a mould.

14 Paint on the leather patches with black edible paint or pen.

Gamer Cupcakes

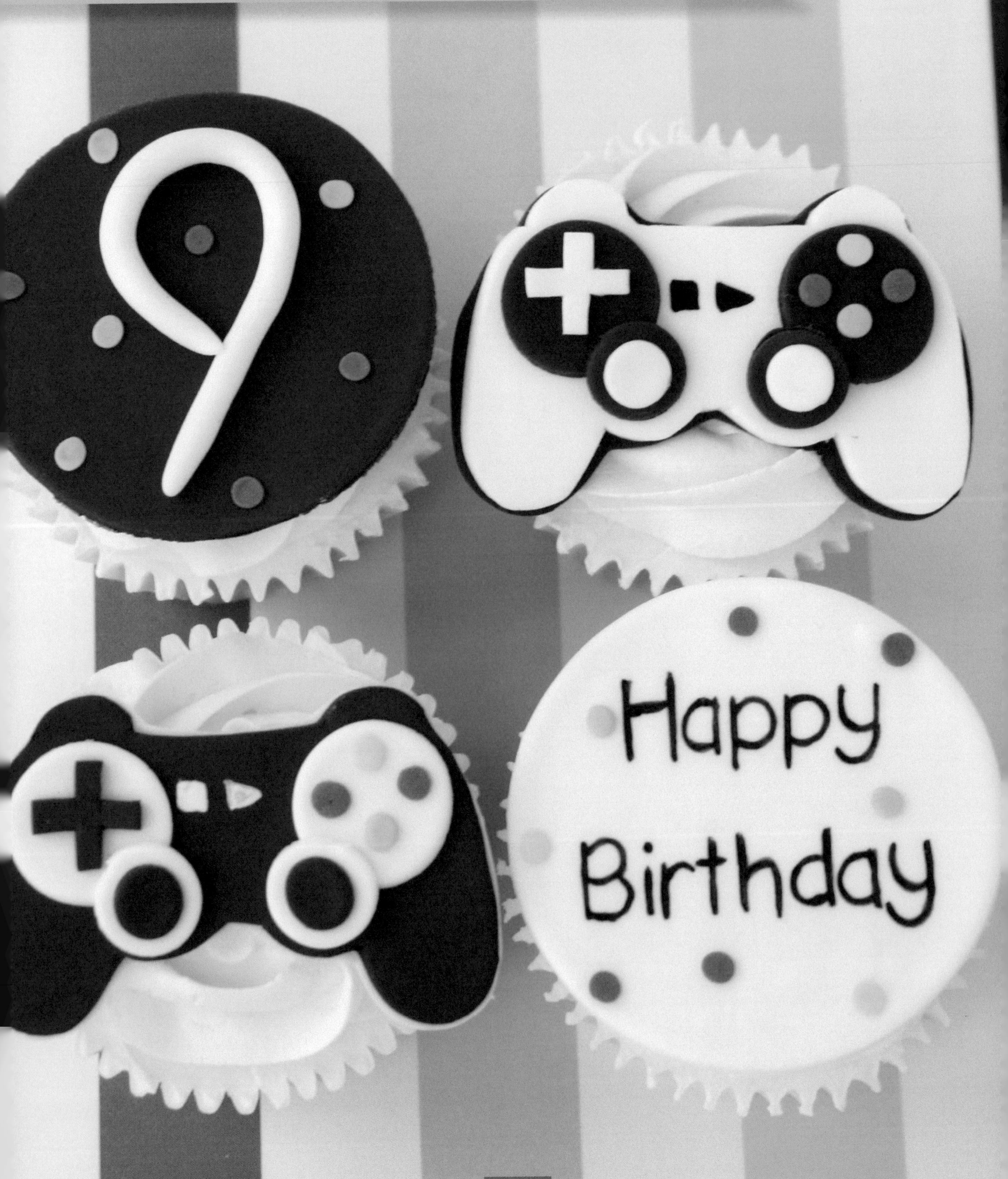

1 If possible, check and take a photo of the handset for birthday boy's favourite game console. Or copy this.

2 Roll out some black modelling paste and carefully cut out a controller shape, as shown.

3 Cut some in black, some in white. Grey is also an option.

4 Add two circles as shown.

5 Cut out a cross using the craft knife.

6 Make four tiny coloured balls and flatten them with the end of your rolling pin.

7 Attach the cross and the coloured buttons.

8 Cut out two white circles, and two smaller black circles.

9 Attach the smaller circles on top of the white ones, and glue to the controller.

10 Roll out some white paste, and place the controller on top. Carefully cut round the controller, leaving a little edge of white paste showing.

11 Paint on the little button details.

12 Make an exact copy of the controller, switching round the colours.

13 Using an edible marker pen, write your message on to a disc of sugarpaste and add a few matching polka dots.

14 Roll out a sausage of paste into the number of the birthday boy's age and add some spots too!

RECIPES ♥ TUTORIALS | Cake & Bake ACADEMY Est. 2014 | RESOURCES ♥ INSPIRATION

The Cute & Easy Cake Toppers Collection is a fantastic range of mini tutorial books covering a wide range of party themes!

Oh Baby!
Cute & Easy Cake Toppers for any Baby Shower, Christening, Birthday or Baby Celebration!

Princesses, Fairies & Ballerinas!
Cute & Easy Cake Toppers for any Princess Party or Girly Celebration!

Puppies and Kittens & Pets, Oh My!
Puppies, Kittens, Bunnies, Pets and more!

Tiny Tea Parties!
Mini Food and Tiny Tea Parties That Look Good Enough To Eat!

Passion for Fashion!
Cute & Easy Cake Toppers! Shoes, Bags, Make-up and more! Mini Fashions That Look good Enough To Eat!

Pirates & Cowboys!
Cute & Easy Cake Toppers for any Pirate Party or Cowboy Celebration!

Cute and Easy Cake Toppers
Brenda Walton from Sugar High shows how to make cute and easy cake topper characters at home!

PLUS:

Easter
Cute & Easy Easter Cake Toppers!

Cake Toppers for Girls!
Tons of girly cake topper cuteness!

Cake Toppers for Men!
Many manly mini cake toppers!

Farmyard Fun!
Tractors, Diggers and Farm Animals Galore!

Circus Time!
All The Fun Of The Big Top!

Jungle Fun!
Lions and Tigers and Monkeys, Oh My!

Xmas Time!
Cute & Easy Xmas Cake Toppers!

and more!

Available in Paperback or instant PDF!

All books are available on Paperback : £6.95 / $10.95

Also available on instant PDF for just £2.95 / $5.95 from: www.cakeandbakeacademy.com

Search on Amazon under 'Cake & Bake Academy' or visit:

www.cakeandbakeacademy.com

13705764R00027

Printed in Poland
by Amazon Fulfillment
Poland Sp. z o.o., Wrocław